The Jaunty Guide to Bitcoin

Michael Rolls

To Whitey

Contents

Michael Rolls

Introduction

This is a book written by me - someone who isn't a computer scientist or mathematician but who has attempted to understand Bitcoin - for people like me - people who are not computer scientists or mathematicians but who want to attempt to understand Bitcoin.

I've avoided going too deep into the complexities because, frankly, the complexities are beyond me. I have sometimes approached them and it is at these moments where you - if you are a Bitcoin expert - are most likely to find an error or two. If you're not a Bitcoin expert and don't want to be, I wouldn't worry about it. Every simplified account of Bitcoin you are likely to find will most probably have an error or two because it is a difficult thing to simplify.

The best advice if you want to grasp it without confusing yourself too much with *computer-cryptocurrency-mathy-stuff* is to jump right in and buy yourself a little bitcoin and learn by using it.

Also, read the rest of this little book.

Part 1: What is Bitcoin?

Bitcoin is internet money. It can be used to pay for goods and services and does not require the involvement of a third party. As of the writing of this book it could not, in all honesty, be used to buy many goods and services. It is not accepted on Amazon or Ebay or by most of the other major online retailers. Because of this Bitcoin continues to be treated as if it were an investment: it attracts the attentions of speculators whilst most people continue to pay for things on the internet with credit cards or through PayPal. There are reasons, however, why this should change and there are reasons for Bitcoin to continue to grow in popularity.

Throughout this book I'll be using the word 'bitcoin' in two different ways. One, to refer to the actual 'coins' (it will become clear later on that these 'coins' are actually strings of numerical data). Two, to refer to the system and community through which bitcoins are mined, traded, and spent. When I refer to this system I'll capitalise the word: Bitcoin and when I refer to the coins I will refer to them as bitcoins.

How Bitcoin is like a Pub

In January 2009 the first bitcoins were produced (they were actually *mined* but we don't need to go into that just yet). They were produced by a mysterious person or persons called Satoshi Nakamoto who has since completely disappeared. This is not suspicious; he/she/they may just be shy.

Satoshi Nakamoto wanted to create a system by which payments could be made on the internet that was as simple and easy as handing £5 to a bloke in the pub for a porn tape. This analogy works quite well. Here are some facts about buying things from a bloke you meet in the pub:

1. The government doesn't know about it unless you or the bloke tells them

2. The other people in the pub can know about it if they care enough to pay attention

3. There's a pretty good chance the stuff you bought is illegal (perhaps it's smuggled booze, dodgy pornography or some drugs)

4. The whole thing is more-or-less anonymous assuming you don't tell everyone your name

5. If you change your mind after you've given the bloke your money he's probably not going to give it back

Before Bitcoin there was no similar way to buy things through the internet. If you tried, a whole load of people *other than you and the bloke* would know about it and most probably take a bit of the money. Paypal, your bank, the credit card issuer and so on and so forth. It would be like going into the pub and instead of handing £5 to the bloke you're trying to buy porn from you instead hand it to a different bloke who then hands it to another bloke who takes a couple percent and records the details of the whole sordid deal and then hands the £5 to the bloke who sends you your porn via two or three other blokes. The whole thing is a very crowded mess.

Here are some facts about paying for stuff from a bloke through the internet with bitcoin:

1. The government doesn't know about it unless you or the bloke tells them

2. The other people in the Bitcoin system can know about it if they care enough to look into it

3. There's a pretty good chance the stuff you bought is illegal

4. The whole thing in more-or-less anonymous assuming you don't tell everyone your name

5. If you change your mind after you've given the bloke your money he's probably not going to give it back

Now you see just how similar Bitcoin is to your local pub. You might wonder why anyone would think this way of doing things is good... if you were buying perfectly legal things why would you want or need to be anonymous? Isn't it better if you're allowed to change your mind and get your money back? Why would you want buying things on the internet to be in any way similar to buying things from some bloke in a dodgy pub?

I hope to answer these questions and more in the coming pages.

Some theory

"Commerce on the internet has come to rely almost exclusively on financial institutions serving as trusted third parties to process electronic payments. While the system works well enough for most transactions, it still suffers from the inherent weaknesses of the trust based model. Completely non-reversible

transactions are not really possible, since financial institutions cannot avoid mediating disputes. The cost of mediation increases transaction costs, limiting the minimum practical transaction size and cutting off the possibility for small casual transactions, and there is a broader cost in the loss of ability to make non-reversible payments for non-reversible services. With the possibility of reversal, the need for trust spreads. Merchants must be wary of their customers, hassling them for more information than they would otherwise need. A certain percentage of fraud is accepted as unavoidable. These costs and payment uncertainties can be avoided in person by using physical currency, but no mechanism exists to make payments over communications channels without a trusted party." - Satoshi Nakamoto

Let's go through this quote from Satoshi Nakamoto and see what he was hoping to achieve by the creation of Bitcoin...

Firstly he identifies an issue; *that commerce on the internet relies on financial institutions serving as trusted third parties.* Instead of having to put your trust in any merchant you happen to buy things from you instead put your trust into Visa or Mastercard or PayPal. The trusted third party.

The advantages of this trusted third party system is that if something goes wrong - if you lose your money for some reason - the trusted third party takes responsibility for that and you can, very possibly, get your money back. This is good. But if it is the only way to pay for things on the internet then *every* exchange will incur the additional costs and complications that are necessary for the trusted third party system.

This means that there is a whole category of buying and selling that isn't cost effective on the internet. Small Casual Transactions.

The costs of mediation increases transaction costs, limiting the minimum practical transaction size and cutting off the possibility for small casual transactions.

Small casual transactions is what Bitcoin is for. You may have read about bitcoin being used to buy Lamborghinis or Private Jets in the papers but those kinds of transactions will most probably always be unusual. Even if Bitcoin becomes the internet currency that everyone uses.

When most people make big purchases they tend to want there to be a trusted third party involved. And we don't mind that there are a few additional costs such as transactions fees.

When it comes to small casual transactions on the other hand we don't really care about having some third party being in on the deal and we certainly don't want additional costs making our small casual transaction a bit less small.

If you want to donate a couple pounds to The Shark Trust because you just watched a clip on YouTube of Chinese people slicing the dorsal fins off sharks it's a bit of an annoyance to have to do that through a third party. Why can't you just send them pounds directly? You don't care if the donation is non-reversible. You don't need a third party for such a transaction.

With the possibility of reversal, the need for trust spreads. Merchants must be wary of their customers, hassling them for more information than they would otherwise need.

The point here is that if you want a transaction to be reversible - perhaps your Lamborghini is faulty - it will be more costly and complicated than a non-reversible one. The merchant who offers such reversible transactions can no longer trust his customers. Customers may buy nice clothes for a night out and then return them the next day. The necessity for a third party arises to either ensure such frauds don't occur or to compensate for it. Such things add costs to the transaction and complicate it.

Questions About Security

Of course, PayPal does make things quite easy. If you see a 'PayPal donate' button on a website it's pretty simple to click it, type in your password and you're done. What advantages does Bitcoin have over PayPal then?

Arguably the main advantage is to do with security.

The advantage certainly isn't anything to do with the complicated procedure of setting up a PayPal account. Getting yourself set-up in Bitcoin is equally cumbersome (but I'll get to that later).

PayPal is linked to your bank account. When there's a shortage of funds in your PayPal account it dips into your bank account to make up the difference. The only thing protecting your bank account then is your PayPal password or PIN number. And it's not very difficult for someone to get a hold of either of those (perhaps through some malware that tracks your keystrokes). And let's face it, your password is probably your kid's date of birth or the name of your dog or 'Password01'.

Credit cards have a similar problem with security: every time you type in your credit card number, expiry date and 'security' number some malware could very easily be recording those details and sending them somewhere. Before you know it your credit card is maxed out by someone you've never heard of going shopping in Vladivostok (or somewhere). Your credit card may not charge you - who knows - but it's a heck of a worry and inconvenience and you don't need this kind of nonsense.

Bitcoin is *much* more secure than both of the payment methods mentioned above. How it's secure is quite complicated. There are things that make Bitcoin secure – things like *private keys, public keys, the blockchain* - for now let's just say it is both much more secure than the alternative methods and potentially much easier to use.

It's also worth considering that there is no other electronic cash system in which your account isn't owned by someone else. Take PayPal, for example: if the company decides that you've been misusing your account it has the power to freeze all of the assets held in the account, without consulting you. You then have to jump through whatever hoops PayPal wants you to jump through to unlock your account and access your own funds again. With Bitcoin you own your Bitcoin account (your Bitcoin *wallet*) and no one can freeze it. It's yours.

There is a problem though; despite the various advantages offered by Bitcoin it is, for the time being, not much more than a theoretical advantage. Bitcoin is not yet a payment method accepted by many retailers. So at the time of writing this book it is not yet a workable alternative to the usual payment methods.

For the time being Bitcoin is not a currency or a payment system because there are not enough people using it as such. At the moment people appear to be treating Bitcoin as an investment.

Is Bitcoin an Investment?

Between November 2013 and today the price of a single bitcoin has fluctuated between $1000 and about $400. And the reason the price has been going up and down is because of people speculating. People are buying into Bitcoin in the hope of it becoming an established and much-used internet currency; in the hope of it becoming more valuable. When news comes that the Chinese government is regulating against the use of Bitcoin the 'investors' get cold feet and sell. Slightly cleverer and more optimistic 'investors' do precisely the opposite. When the news comes that Overstock.com is now accepting bitcoin the first 'investors' get their balls back and buy bitcoins.

And this pattern of behaviour will continue for as long as Bitcoin is a potential currency.

> *"It might make sense just to get some in case it catches on. If enough people think the same way, that becomes a self fulfilling prophecy. Once it gets bootstrapped, there are so many applications if you could effortlessly pay a few cents to a website as easily as dropping coins in a vending machine."*
> – Satoshi Nakamoto in 2009

Yes, you can treat Bitcoin as an investment if you wish. You can buy some bitcoins and, if Bitcoin becomes more popular and ends up being the much-used internet currency it was intended to be, then perhaps you'll make a little profit. Perhaps a lot of profit if any of the predictions listed here come to pass:

"If bitcoin grows into something bigger – a useful reserve currency, then watch out: Its value will far exceed $400,000... I personally think that bitcoin is already superior to gold. Its role as currency is yet to be determined, but over the next decade, being Gold 2.0 will suffice considering that it would represent a more than 3,000 times return." - Former Facebook executive Chamath Palihapitiya.

"Small bull case scenario for Bitcoin is a 400bn USD market cap, so 40,000 USD a coin, but I believe it could be much larger. When this will happen, if it happens, I don't know, but if it happens, it will probably happen much faster than anyone imagines." - Cameron Winklevoss of the Winklevoss twins.

In my opinion, you should buy a bitcoin (or some of one, or two). If they become incredibly valuable; that's good. If they don't become incredibly valuable but do become the method by which things are bought on the Internet, they will be useful. If neither of these things happen and the bitcoins dwindle away and become utterly worthless, bad luck. At least you didn't spend your lifesavings on them, did you?!

Part 2: How Bitcoin Works

"Total circulation will be 21,000,000 coins. It'll be distributed
to network nodes when they make blocks, with the amount cut in half
every 4 years.

first 4 years: 10,500,000 coins
next 4 years: 5,250,000 coins
next 4 years: 2,625,000 coins
next 4 years: 1,312,500 coins
etc..." – Satoshi Nakamoto

There will never be any more than 21,000,000 bitcoins. This is guaranteed by MATHS and COMPUTERS and PEOPLE WHO KNOW ABOUT MATHS AND COMPUTERS. At the moment (February 2014) there are about 12,000,000 bitcoins. So about half of the eventual total are in circulation or, more likely, hoarded away in the Bitcoin wallets of early adopters.

This limit on how many bitcoins can exist is a bulwark but not a guarantee against deflation. If no-one will exchange anything for a bitcoin then it's probably worth nothing and not worth having.

A question you might reasonably ask is where do they come from? The answer is not 'The Royal Mint'.

Where Bitcoins Come From

In the beginning there was Satoshi Nakamoto and he/she/them/it wanted to make a virtual currency. Such things had been attempted in the past. In fact, the famous big-shot Nobel Laureate free market economist Milton Friedman had said as long ago as 1999 that a virtual currency would be a good idea - '*one thing that hasn't been developed yet is a reliable e-currency*'.

In 2008 Satoshi Nakamoto published a paper explaining Bitcoin (and I've quoted from this liberally throughout this book) and 'mined' the first bitcoins. The mining process is where they come from.

Mining: imagine you come across some land where oil squirts from the ground unprompted. You are happy to discover it and collect it up in a bucket and you continue to do so for as long as the oil continues to spill forth.

You don't mind because all you need are a couple cheap buckets and the only effort you expend is replacing the bucket every time it fills up.

One day the oil stops squirting and just spills out of the ground in a puddle so you have to put down some plastic to stop it soaking into the sand and you have to funnel it into the bucket. It's a little more expense and a bit more effort but you don't mind.

One day the oil stops altogether so you buy a shovel and start digging. Then you have to buy a pump to pump the oil out of the hole.

As it becomes more difficult to get to the oil you continue to purchase more expensive and specialised equipment. Before long you have a specially built rig set up and it's pumping an ever dwindling supply of oil from the ground.

It's hard work but, on the other hand you are rich now and it seems like the more oil you mine the more valuable it is.

Bitcoins do not come from the ground. They are mined but the use of the word 'mine' merely displays the poetic bent of the minds of the technologists who invented cryptocurrencies. What the word actually refers to is the process by which computers uncover bitcoins.

The computers called miners engage in a process of work through which they verify bitcoin transactions, as an incentive to engage in this work there is the possibility that any computer engaging in such work may be rewarded in bitcoins. Any of the computers mining could be the one to earn the reward.

The first bitcoins were relatively easy to mine. Satoshi Nakamoto just, sort of, *did it*. He set his mining program going and the computer produced some bitcoins.

The mining process, however, becomes more difficult over time.
"As computers get faster and the total computing power applied to mining bitcoins increases, the difficulty increases proportionally to keep the total new production constant. Thus it is known in advance how many bitcoins will be created every year in the future"
– Satoshi Nakamoto

If you wanted to mine bitcoins today you would have to buy a specialised mining computer that can engage in more-and-more labour-intensive work that is necessary for the mining of bitcoins. It will need to be left switched on for long periods and your electricity bill will be terrifying and it probably won't earn a bitcoin anyway.

It would take your household Commodore 64 a trillian-trillian-billion decades to mine just one bit of a bitcoin! And by that time humans will be using something else anyway. (I made this up, but you get the idea).

More Stuff About Mining

Whenever a miner performs a confirmation of a Bitcoin transaction he, in doing so, adds the data of that transaction to something called the blockchain. The blockchain is a big long chain of data. It's divided into Blocks. So is called the blockchain. The details of every Bitcoin transaction make up the blockchain. And anyone in the Bitcoin system can look at the blockchain. Every transaction is therefore visible to anyone who cares. You can see which bitcoins were transferred from where to where.

Once a transaction is confirmed and added to the blockchain it is set in stone and can never be changed or deleted in any way. It is a part of history. It is this process of confirming transactions, locking them and adding them to the blockchain that earns miners their newly minted bitcoins.

The system is set up so that the later in the history of Bitcoin the miners are mining the more work they have to do to eventually uncover any bitcoins.

In roughly 2105 when the final bitcoin is due to be mined a *lot* of miners will be doing a *lot* of work before one of them earns (mines) it.

After the last bitcoin is mined the miners will continue to do their work, the reward, however, will not be mined bitcoins, it will instead come from the (voluntary) transaction fees Bitcoin users choose to pay when they spend some bitcoin.

Anyway, I hope some of that is clear to you - it's slightly clearer to me. However, let's remember that you don't have to know how money is made to use it and spend it. You didn't have a guided tour of the Royal Mint before you spent your first £5 note after all. So we'll move on to how you can get and spend bitcoins.

Part 3: How To Start Using Bitcoin

First, you'll need a Bitcoin wallet

Then, you'll need some bitcoins to put in the wallet

Then, you'll need to find places to use your bitcoins

1. Getting a Bitcoin wallet
You can sign up for an online Bitcoin wallet from somewhere like https://Blockchain.com. This is easy; you go to the website, you type in your email address and Blockchain.com gives you a Bitcoin wallet address. A Bitcoin wallet address looks like this:

1LqEkGfGkZbw5sj96P6k4ux3e5o7kWKY9Q

When someone wants to send you some bitcoin they will enter your wallet address as the recipient and the amount they want to send from their wallet. They'll click send and after a little time the amount will disappear from their wallet and appear in your wallet.

It's worth pointing out that the amount of time it takes for a transaction to complete depends on how many 'confirmations' it is subject to. 'Confirmations' are the things that make sure you don't do something dodgy like try to double-spend your bitcoins. If it's a large transaction you would want a decent amount of confirmations to be done because it is through these confirmations that a transaction is shown to be legitimate. If you're only receiving or sending a small amount then the number of confirmations can be small and the transaction will be completed quickly. (Remember, by the way, it is the miners who confirm transactions and it is by doing this that they hope to earn/mine free bitcoins.)

It is generally recommended that you should not use an online wallet as your main one (wallet hosting companies have been subject to the occasional bitcoin heist). The alternative is to have some Bitcoin wallet software on your computer. This wallet would be on your computer and would store your bitcoins on your own hard-drive rather than on the server of https://blockchain.com (or wherever).

This is also easy: you go somewhere like https://multibit.org/ download the software and install it on your computer. The wallet on your computer will let you create a lot of Bitcoin wallet addresses – this is good because it is advisable to not use the same one too many times. Make sure to backup your wallet(s) regularly on an external hard-drive just in case your computer gets stolen or your hard-drive breaks.

Anyway, here's what I do: I have an online wallet at https://blockchain.com but I regularly send any bitcoin I have there to a wallet on my computer. The blockchain.com address is the one I hand out and stuff; it's the address you read a couple paragraphs ago. The other wallet addresses I don't give out at all.

2. Getting some bitcoin

You could publish your Bitcoin wallet address in the classified section of Private Eye and hope a rich benefactor sends you some for free!

You could make a QR code out of your Bitcoin address and stick it on lampposts all around town in the hope that one of the rich benefactors that swarm our towns and cities scans it, realises it's a Bitcoin wallet address, and, having many bitcoins themselves, decides to send you some for free and for no reason.

These two options are unlikely to work depending as they do on the existence of bitcoin-rich benefactors who like throwing money around.

The way you'll most likely get some bitcoin is by buying some. You can go to somewhere like https://bitbargain.co.uk/ (such places may require you to jump through some hoops to set-up an account, others may not depending on how much they care about security) and exchange money for bitcoin.

This in itself was a bit of a cumbersome and long-winded process for me and I don't want to go into it. But once it's done, it's done. In time, one hopes, the process by which normal people (i.e. not Bitcoin fanatics) can exchange their usual currency for bitcoin will become much, much easier.

Another way to get bitcoin is to buy it from a bloke in the pub. By which I mean you can go to somewhere like https://localbitcoins.com/

where you can contact a local bitcoin seller and arrange to meet him or her in your local pub. You can meet, hand over some cash and he or she will send you bitcoin. Easy.

3. Buy Some Stuff

What some companies like to do, it seems to me, is to get some free advertising by announcing that they now accept bitcoin. They will keep doing this for as long as 'company accepts bitcoin' is considered news. The moment bitcoin is widely accepted is the moment 'company accepts bitcoin' ceases to be considered news.

Anyway, now you have some bitcoin you may want to buy some stuff. Alternatively, you may wish to hold on to your bitcoin in the hope of it becoming incredibly valuable. If you choose to buy stuff here is a very, very short list of places you can buy things from with bitcoin.

- www.overstock.com for various things (bedsheets are a big seller with the bitcoin crowd, apparently)
- www.fiverr.com - for pretty much any service a person can sell for a fiver or more
- www.takeaway.com - for takeaway food
- www.8ballbikes.co.uk - for bicycle stuff
- www.girlmeetsdress.com - for dresses
- www.belovedshirts.com - for shirts
- www.jolioriginals.com - for Italian leather IPod cases and thingamajigs
- www.cloudyskyleatherworks.com - for more leather stuff
- www.fangamer.net - games

- www.orbit-streetwear.com - 'street' wear... whatever the hell that is

- www.lurings.com - earrings, probably

For a much longer list go to www.shopify.co.uk where you will find 75,000 merchants who accept bitcoin. Including a taxi driver in Hertfordshire and a man with a van in East London.

Part 4: Infrequently Asked Questions

Is Bitcoin Really Inflation-Proof?

"The fact that new coins are produced means the money supply increases by a planned amount, but this does not necessarily result in inflation. If the supply of money increases, prices remain stable. If it does not increase as fast as demand, there will be deflation and early holders of the money will see its value increase" – Satoshi Nakamoto

That's the theory. So it looks like deflation might be more of a worry....

Won't Loss of Wallets and the Finite Amount of Bitcoins Create Excessive Deflation?

It could happen. As a result of there being a limited supply of bitcoins and because people - forgetful as they are - tend to lose stuff there is a chance that the supply of bitcoin will sort of dwindle away. If a Bitcoin user loses his wallet, his money is gone forever, unless he finds it again. The bloke who recently lost his $9,000,000 worth of bitcoin when he threw out an old hard drive has to accept that they are gone (unless someone spends a lot of time and energy digging around for the hard drive in the city dump). And not just to him; it's gone completely out of circulation, rendered utterly inaccessible to anyone. As people will lose their wallets, the total number of bitcoins will slowly decrease.

Bitcoin, then, has a unique problem. Whereas most currencies inflate over time, Bitcoin will probably do the opposite. And as more and more bitcoins get lost in the city dump or get left on USB sticks that fall into lakes or somewhere the laws of supply and demand suggest that the value of bitcoin will probably continually rise.

No one really knows anything about this sort of constant-deflation situation…with most currencies it would create a problem: if £1 can suddenly buy a castle, how the hell do you buy a bag of Jelly Babies? It's not very practical. Bitcoin, however, avoids this problem by being infinitely divisible.

How Divisible are Bitcoins?

Bitcoins can be divided up and the little bits of them can be used. This sort of solves the 'lost bitcoins' problem because even if loads of people drop their Bitcoin wallets into the ocean the remaining bitcoins can still be divided up and used.

A bitcoin can be divided down to 8 decimal places. 0.00000001 BTC is the smallest amount that can be handled in a transaction at the moment but, if necessary, the whole system can be modified so that smaller amounts can be used.

What Do I Call the Various Denominations of Bitcoin?

I have no idea… and there doesn't seem to be much agreement on it yet. Here, however, are some of the terms that are sometimes used:

1 BTC = 1 bitcoin

0.01 BTC = 1 cBTC = 1 centibitcoin

0.001 BTC = 1 mBTC = 1 millibitcoin

0.000 001 BTC = 1 µBTC = 1 microbitcoin

0.000 000 01 BTC = 1 satoshi

I suppose we'll only know what to say when we have to start mentioning the things in normal everyday life (as opposed to Bitcoin-fanatic-on-a-Libertarian-website life… which is an altogether different thing).

Can I Withdraw My Bitcoins at an ATM/Cashpoint?

Crikey, yes you can. You can deposit money and change it to bitcoins or vice-versa. And the ATMs are popping up at such a rate that one probably popped up at the end of your street in the time it took you to read this sentence (assuming that you live in a sufficiently trendy area). The things are so cheap and easy to set up you can probably buy one and put it in your kitchen if you want to.

Can I Insure My Bitcoins?

Things are moving fast in the world of Bitcoin. There was no company offering bitcoin insurance a week ago but now there is. A company called Elliptic based in London. Maybe in another week it will be gone, maybe it won't. Who knows.

Where Does the Value of Bitcoin Come From?

Bitcoins have value for as long as they are of use and because they are scarce. Beyond that they're not 'backed' by anything. But nor are pounds since we left the Gold Standard. Bitcoins have value because people think they do; if people en masse decide that a bitcoin is worth precisely nothing then that's what it will be worth. So it goes.

Part 5: A Mt Gox Diary

Before 2014, if you, a person who had read about Bitcoin in the press, had decided you wanted to find out more and try Bitcoin, you would have done a search on Google. When you wanted to find a site on which you could trade some bitcoin you would have done what people who use Google do: trust the sites that appear at the top of the Google search and those that look most professional.

The Bitcoin exchange that appeared at the top would have been Mt Gox. And it looked good too. A quick skim of a few columns written about Bitcoin would have told you that the *biggest* and *most successful* Bitcoin exchange is Mt Gox. We respect *big and successful*. And, for some reason, we trust *big and successful* too. To the casual observer Mt Gox may have looked like the Next Big Thing. Why would you do any deeper research?

Why indeed. Mt Gox is dead and gone now and it's taken a lot of people's money with it.

This chapter is a late addition to the book. It's a sort of Diary of the Death of Mt Gox. Hopefully you'll get some useful information from it. Mt Gox, after all, is not the first Bitcoin exchange to disappear with people's bitcoins. And it might not be the last.

If there is one lesson to learn it might be this: whilst Bitcoin is still a new technology, you should make sure any website you trust your money to has, at the very least, a good reputation in the Bitcoin community.

Mt Gox did not have a good reputation amongst those who knew what to look for...

Before February 2014

Back in June 2011 there was some suspicion that Mt Gox didn't have the amount of bitcoin it should have and the CEO (Mark Karpeles) moved a large number of bitcoins from one wallet to another to prove Mt Gox's solvency (remember: bitcoin transactions are public so this movement of funds was visible to everyone in the community).

From around October 2013 transferring bitcoins to US Dollars through Mt Gox began to be a bit of a hit-and-miss process. Sometimes the requested transfer wouldn't happen and sometimes it would take a long time to happen. Some people would try and try over and over again to withdraw their bitcoins without much luck.

Mt Gox answers complaints very slowly. And the answers that come are uninformative.

Some people think it's a software issue. Some think it's a solvency issue.

February 2014

February is when everything hit the proverbial fan. Presumably, those who had spotted the warning signs had abandoned Mt Gox already if they were able to. Increasingly, though, even if you knew there was a big problem you would find that your bitcoins were trapped in Mt Gox and you couldn't get them out.

You might suspect that far from being trapped, your bitcoins might not be there at all. If your bitcoins are not there, where are they?

1st February: the Bank of China ends all Bitcoin trading in China. Many investors get cold feet and sell their bitcoins. The stampede of investors attempting to withdraw from Mt Gox, however, hit a problem: a lot of their bitcoins are stuck. Enough so that far more people start to care about the nature of Mt Gox's problems.

7th February: Mt Gox disables all Bitcoin withdrawals citing technical problems as the reason. They later say that the problem in question is a Bitcoin protocol problem. The Bitcoin community quickly identify this as nonsense because the problem cited, the 'transaction malleability bug', is widely known (and has been for a while) and it's not really a problem.

The transaction malleability bug had, in fact, been fixed in the Bitcoin system. Mt Gox, however, had not updated it's processes accordingly. This failure may have led to Mt Gox having a system that was susceptible to 'transaction malleability attacks' – attacks whereby someone uses the bug to claim to have not received bitcoin that has been sent to him.

15th February: Mt Gox ceases trading for six hours for 'debugging'. Everyone suspects (knows) this is nonsense.

19th February: Mt Gox moves offices. It seems they thought there were 'security issues' because there were a couple of people on the street outside with 'where's our bitcoin?' placards.

The office move is a strange thing to do in the middle of a crisis. The situation by this point can definitely be called a crisis. The new office is a little 'rent-a-room' place in a Tokyo backstreet. It has a phone-line. If you call you get to listen to some Muzak, nothing more.

20th February: Mt Gox sells a huge amount of bitcoin. They also claim that their failure to release any information about what's going on is due to the office move.

24th February: a report is leaked that says there has been a 'cold storage leak' resulting in the loss of 744,408 bitcoin, that Mt Gox is insolvent and that the leak has been leaking for years without anyone noticing. Any questions about what kind of 'cold storage' springs leaks go unanswered.

The Mt Gox website goes offline. Everyone distances themselves from Mt Gox.

<u>28th February</u>: Mt Gox files for bankruptcy protection. 64 million US dollars and 850,000 bitcoin are missing.

After February 2014

No one really knows what happened. The missing money is about 7% of all existing bitcoin. So, it's a lot. A leading theory is that CEO Mark Karpeles has been withdrawing bitcoin from Mt Gox since 2011. Another is that Mt Gox has been subject to multiple attacks whereby the weaknesses in its' systems were exploited. Another is that Mt Gox has lost the keys to some of its' wallets and so all the money is still there; it's just that no-one can get to it.

That last theory is almost certainly wishful thinking on the part of some who have lost money.

Part 6: The End of the Book

All that information may now be a jumble in your brain and, apparently, of little use. Don't worry though, it's probably all settled nicely in your subconscious and will furnish you with useful nuggets of info as you attempt to get a Bitcoin wallet and then buy a dress from www.girlmeetsdress.com.

In fact, I would go as far as to say that your subconscious brain now has a firm grasp of all things Bitcoin (except for the complicated stuff that hardly anyone needs to know and which I couldn't tell you even if I wanted to) and you can, with confidence, begin experimenting with the thing. Good luck!

ABOUT THE AUTHOR

Michael Rolls writes about many other things he knows very little about. Such writings can be found at www.michaelrolls.com

Tips Accepted Here

www.ingramcontent.com/pod-product-compliance
Lightning Source LLC
Chambersburg PA
CBHW060502210326
41520CB00015B/4063